Minister Training Manual

by Bishop Gillis and Gwendolyn Thomas

RoseDog Books
PITTSBURGH, PENNSYLVANIA 15238

RoseDog Books
585 Alpha Drive
Pittsburgh, PA 15238
Visit our website at *www.rosedogbookstore.com*

ISBN: 978-1-4809-1706-4
eISBN: 978-1-4809-1684-5

BISHOP GILLIS & GWENDOLYN THOMAS
World International Revival Center

(House Of Hope)
103 Elm Street
Pensacola, FL 32506

TRAINING MANUAL

2 Timothy 2:15
Study to show thyself approved unto God, a workman that needeth not to be ashamed, rightly dividing the word of truth.

Words of Encouragement

We here at World International Revival Center believing in equipping our ministers with the word of God, teaching and training them to be efficient in ministry and in the word of God. We believe in training champions. We also believe in taking the ministry to the next level. We believe in pushing the young men and women to the next level in God. Our job here at World International Revival Center, is to make sure that each student is equipped with the necessary training that it takes to minister in their office. Each individual that comes to us has different talents and skills, we here at World International Revival Center, believe in bringing them to their full potential that God has placed them in. So if you believe that you are that person and up to the challenge, we want to train you, so God Bless You,

From The Staff,
World International Revival Center
W.I.R.C. (House Of Hope).

Prayer
Is an invocation or act that seeks to activate a report rapport with a Deity or Spiritual Entity through deliberate communication.

Prepare
Make ready to use or consideration.

Preparation
The action of making ready or being made ready for use.

Purpose
The reason for which something exists or is done, made used, an intended or desired results; end, aim, goal.

Perfection
The state or quality of being or becoming perfect.

Bible Training for Christians

2 Tim. 2:2; And the things that thouhast heard of me among many witnesses, the same commit thou to faithful men, who shall be able to teach other also.

The Church has the responsibility to safeguard the true and original apostolic doctrine found in scripture and commit it to others, without compromise or corruption. This implies the necessity of Biblical instruction within the church.

1) The Bible gives the following reasons for Biblical or Theological Training, whether in home, church, or school.
   (a) To entrust the gospel of Christ to faithful believers, in order that they may know (2 Tim. 3:15), guard (2 Tim. 1:14 notes), and teach the true Biblical faith (1 Tim. 4:6,11) (2 Tim. 2:2), and righteous standards (see, Rom. 6:17); (note, 1 Tim. 6:3).
   (b) To show students the vital necessity to contend for the faith that was once for all entrusted to the saints (Jude 3, notes), and to give them the means by which to defend it aganist all false theologies (see, Acts 20:31); note, (Gal. 1:9); note, (1 Tim. 4:1; 6:3-4); (Tit. 1:9).
   (c) To lead students into continual growth in charcter, through Godly teaching. (1 Tim. 6:3); (Josh. 1:8); (Ps. 1:2-3; 119:97-100); (Matt. 28:20); (John 17:14-18); (1 Thess. 4:1); (1 Tim. 1:5,

note; 1 Tim. 4:7, 16); (2 Tim. 3:16). (d). To equip students to strenghten and bring to maturity other believers, so that together they may reflect Christ's image in the home, the Local Church and the Body of Christ. (Eph. 4:11-16).

(e)　To bring students to a deeper understanding and experience of God's Kingdom on earth and its conflict aganist Stan's power (Eph. 6:10-18).

(f)　To motivate students, through the eternal truths of the gospel, to be whole to be wholeheartedly committed to evangelizing the lost, and preaching the gospel to all nation, the power of hte Holy Spirit (Matt. 28:18-20); (Mark 16:15-20).

(g)　To deepen students experience of Christ's love, personal fellowship, and gift of the Spirit (John 17:3,21,26); (Eph. 3:18-19); by urging them to fellow the leading of the in dwelling Holy Spirit (Rom. 8:14). By bring them into the Baptism in the Holy Spirit (Acts 2:4), and by teaching them to pray, (Matt. 6:9 note), fast (Matt. 6:16 note); and worship as they long for the glorious appearing of Jesus Christ with the Spiritual intensity of New Testament Saints (2 Tim. 4:8); (Tit. 2:13).

2)　It is obvious from these purpose of Biblical training, that instruction must be done only by those who are fervently loyal to Scipture as God's fully inspired word (2 Tim. 1:13-14), and to the Holy Spirit and His Ministry of truth, righteousness, and power (2 Tim. 1:14).

3)　Note that true Biblical training emphasizes true righteousness (i.e., knowing, being, and doing), rather than mere apprehension of Biblical facts or truth. The great doctrines revealed in scripture are redemptive truths, not academic one, as issue involving life or death, they demand a personal response and decision from both teacher and students (James 2:17); see (Phil. 1:9).

APOSTLES

A person personally commissioned by Christ to represent Him. (Matt. 10:1-4).

Apostles

The title "Apostle" is applied to certain leaders in the New Testament. The verb (apostello); means to send someone on a special mission, as a messenger and personal representative to the one who sends him. The title is used by Christ, (Heb. 3:1); the twelve desciples, (Matt. 10:2); and others, (Acts 14:4,14); (Rom. 16:7); (Gal. 1:19; 2:8-9); (1 Thess. 2:6-7).

1. The term "Apostle" was used in the New Testament in a general sense for a commissioned representative of a church, such as the first Christ Missionaries. Therefore in the New Testament, apostles referred to any messenger appointed and sent as a missionary or for some other special responsibility. They were men who manifested extraordinary spiritual leadership, were anointed with power to confront directly the power of darkness and to confirm the gospel with miracles. They were dedicated to establishing churches according to apostolic truth and purity. These itinerant servants risked their lives for the name of the Lord Jesus Christ and advancement of the gospel. (Acts 11:21-26; 13:50; 14:19-22; 15: 25-26). They were spirit filled men of faith and prayer. (Acts 11:23-25; 13:2-5, 46-52; 14:1-7;14.21-23).

2. Apostles in the general sense remain essential to God's purpose in the church. If churches cease to send out spirit filled persons, then the spread of the gospel into all the worldwill be hindered. On the

3

other hand, as long as the church produces and send such peoples, it will fulfill its missionary task, and remain faithful to the Lord's Great commission. (Matt. 28:18-20).

3. The term "Apostle" is also used in a special sense, referring to those who saw Jesus after His resurrection, and were personally commissioned by the resurrected Lord to preach the gospel, and establish the church, the twelve disciples and Paul. They possessed a unique authority within the church, that related to divine revelation and the original gospel message that can no longer exist in anyone today. (Eph. 2:20). Thus the office of apostles in this specialized sense is unique and unrepeatable. The original apostles can have no successors. (1 Cor. 15:8).

4. A primary task of the New Testament apostles, was to establish churches and to ensure that they were founded on or restored to sincere devotion to Christ, and the New Testament faith. (John 21:15-17); (1 Cor. 12:28); (2 Cor. 11:2-3); (Eph. 4:11-12); (Phil. 1:17). This task involved two main burdens:

   (a) An urgent God given desire to maintain the church's purity and its seperation from sin and the world. (1 Cor. 5:1-5); (2 Cor. 6:14-18); (Jas. 2:14-26); (1 Pet. 2:11; 4:1-5); (1 John 2:1, 15-17; 3:3-10).

   (b) A continuing burden to proclaim the New Testament gospel and to defend it aganist heresy, new theological trends and false teachers. (Rom. 16:17); (1 Cor. 11:2); (2 Cor. 11:3-4,14); (Gal. 1:9); (2 Pet. 2:1-3); (1 John 4:1-6); (2 John 1:7-11); (Jude 1:3-4,12-13).

5. Although the first apostles who laid the church's foundation have no successors. The church today is still dependent on their words, message and faith. The church must obey and remain faithful to

4

their original writings. To reject the inspired revelation of the apostles, is to cease being a church according to the Biblical pattern, and to reject the Lord Himself. (John 16:13-15); (1 Cor. 14:36-38); (Gal. 1:9-11). On the other hand, to believe the apostolic message obey it, and guard it aganist all distortion; is to remain true to the Holy Spirit. (Acts 20:28); (2 Tim. 1:14). And to guarantee God's continued life, blessing, and presence within the church. (Eph. 2:20).

APOSTLE

Apostle in the New Testament, this word means; one sent forth, a delegate, envoy, or messenger, especially God's messengers. The term is first used in connection with the twelve, a group of highly honored believers chosen by Jesus to assist Him in His evangelical mission in Palestine. In addition to those, it is used of Mathias, Barnabas, Paul, and Jesus. On this basis of (2 Cor. 8:23); (Phil. 2:35), and early extra bibical references, soave scholars feel that there was a much wider circle of christian messengers and teachers who were called by the name apostle.

THOSE DESIGNATED AS APOSTLE

The Twelve

(Matt. 10:1) - And when he had called unto him his twelve disciples, he gave them the power aganist unclean spirits, to cast them out, and to heal all manner of disease. Now the names of the twelves apostles are these; The first Simon, who was called Simon Peter, and Andrews his brother; James the son of Zebedee, and John his brother; Philip, and Bartholomew, Thomas and Matthew the publican; James the son of Alpheus, and Lebbaeus, whose surname was call Thaddeus, and Simon the canaanite, and Judas Iscariot who also betrayed him.

{see:}; (Mark 3:14; 6:30; Luke 6:13; 9:1; Acts 1:2, 26: and individual articles on these apostles).

A POSSIBLE "CLASS" OF APOSTLE

(2 Cor. 8:23); Whether any do enquire of Ti'tus, he is my partner and fellow helper concerning you: or our brethren be enquired of, they are messengers of the churches, and the glory of Christ.

(Phil. 2:25); Yet I supposed it necessary to send to you E-paph-ro-di'tus, my brother, and companion in labour, and fellowsoldier, but your messenger, and he that ministered to my wants.

DIVINE APPOINTMENT

(Ex. 4:12-13); Now therefore go, and I will be with thy mouth, and teach thee what thou shalt say.

(v13.) And He said, 0 my Lord, send, I pray thee, by the hand of him whom thou wilt send.

(Rom. 1:1); Paul, a servant of Jesus Christ, called to be an apostle, seperated unto the gospel of God.

Cor. 1:21); Now he which stablisheth us with you in Christ, and hath anointed us, is God.

(2 Cor. 2:15-17); For we are unto God a sweet savour of Christ, in them that are saved, and in them that perish:
(v16); To the one we are the savour of death; unto death; and

to the other the savour of life unto life. And who is sufficient for these things?

(v17); For we are not as many, which corrupt the word of God: but as of sincerity, but as of God, in the sight of God speak we in Christ.

(2 Cor. 5:20); Now then we are ambassadors for Christ, as though God did beseech you by us: we pray you in Christ's stead, be ye reconciled to God.

(Gal. 1:1); Paul, an apostle, (not of men, neither by man, but by Jesus Christ, and God the Father, who raised him from the dead;)

(1 Tim. 4:14); Neglect not the gift that is in thee, which was given thee by prophecy, with the laying on of the hands of the presbytery.

APOSTLE
TO SEND OFF

Chief disciple of Christ, the word appears about 80 times in the NT, limited to certain men of the first generation of the church and missionaries of the gospel. The first twelve apostles sent out by Jesus are name in (Mark 3:14-19) and elsewhere, Others also are considered apostles including Paul, James, Barnabas, Mattias, and in some groupings Junias, Andronicus, and Silvanus. Subsequently many claimed the title, which the church desired to limit to those who had seen Jesus and had first hand knowledge of the resurrection, who had the attributes called the signs of an apostle, and were fully committed to the church.

Matt. 10:2 . . . . .Names Of The Twelve Apostles,
Luke 11:49 . . . . .Send Them Prophets And Apostles,

Rom. 1:1 . . . . .Called To Be An Apostle,

Rom 11:13 . . . . .Apostles Of The Gentiles,

1 Cor. 15:9 . . . . .Not Meet To Be Called An Apostle,

2Cor. 12:11 . . . . .Very Chiefest Apostle,

Gal. 1:19 . . . . .Others Of The Apostles Saw I none,

Gal. 2:8 . . . . .Apostleship Of The Circumcision,

Eph, 4:11 . . . . .He Gave Some Apostles;

lTim. 2:7; 2Tim. 1:11 . . . . .And An Apostle,

DESIGNATED AS APOSTLES

MATTH IAS
(Acts 1:26); And they gave forth their lots; and the lot fell upon Matthias; and he was numbered with the eleven apostles.

BARNABAS
(1 Cor. 9:5); Have we not power to lead about a sister, a wife, as well as other apostles, and as the brethren of the Lord, and Ce'phas?

(Gal. 2:9); And when James, Ce'phas, and John, who seemed to be pillars, perceived the grace that was given unto me, they gave to me and Bar'na-bas the right hands of fellowship; that we should go unto the heathen, and they unto the circumcision.

PAUL
(Rom. 1:1); Paul, a servant of Jesus Christ, called to be an apostle, separated unto the gospel of God.,

(Ga1.1:1); Paul, an apostle, (not of men, neither by man, but by Jesus Christ, and God the Father, who raised him from the dead;)

JESUS

(Heb. 3:1); WHEREFORE, holy brethren, partakers of the heavenly calling, consider the Apostle and High Priest of our profession, Christ Jesus;

PROPHETS

An inspired messenger called by God to declare His will (Ezra 5:2).

Prophets

Prophets were believers who spoke under the direct impulse of the Holy Spirit in the name of God, and whose main concern was the spiritual life and purity of the church. Under the new covenant they were raised up and empowered by the Holy Spirit to bring a message from God to His peoples. (Acts 2:17; 4:8; 28:4).

1. Old Testament prophets are foundational for understanding the Prophetic Ministry in the early church. Their primary task was to speak a word of God by the spirit, in order to encourage God's people to remain faithful to their covenant relationship. They also at times, predicted the future as the spirit reveal it to them. Christ and the Apostles served as examples of the Old Testament idea. (Acts 3:22-23; 13:1-2).

2. Prophets functioned with the New Testament Church in the following ways:
    (a) They were spirit filled proclaimers, and interpreters of the word of God; to warn, exhort, comfort, and edify. (Acts 2:14-36; 3:12-26); (1 Cor. 12:10; 14:3).
    (b) They were to excercise the gift of prophecy.
    (c) They were at times seers. (1 Chr. 29:29). Who foretold the future. (Acts 11:28; 21:10-11).
    (d) Like the Old Testament Prophets, the New Testament Prophets

were to expose sin, proclaim righteousness, warn of judgment to come, and combat worldliness, and lukewarmness among God's peoples. (Luke 1:14-17). Because of their message of righteousness, Prophets and their Ministry can expect rejection by many in the churches during time of lukewarmness and apostasy.

3. The Prophet's character, burden, desire, and ability included:
   (a) A zeal for church purity. (John 17:15-17); (1 Cor. 6:9-11); (Gal. 5:22-25).
   (b) A deep sensitivity to evil, and the capacity to identify, define, and hate unrighteousness. (Rom. 12:9); (Heb. 1:9).
   (c) A keen understanding of the danger of false teachings. (Matt. 7:15; 24:11,24); (Gal. 1:9) (2 Cor. 11:12-15).
   (d) An inherent dependence on God's word to validate the Prophet's message. (Luke 4:17-19); (1 Cor. 15:3-4); (2 Tim. 3:16); (1 Peter 4:11).
   (e) A concern for the spiritual success of God's Kingdom and a sharing in the feeling of God. (Matt. 21:11-13; 23:37); (Luke 13:34); (John 2:14-17); (Acts 20: 27-31).

4. The Prophets message are: Not to be regarded as infallible. Their message are subject to the evolution of the church other Prophets and God's word. The congregation is required to discern and test, whether their witness is from God. (1 Cor. 14:29-33); (1 John 4:1).

5. Prophets continue to be essential to God's purpose for the church. A church that rejects God's Prophets will be a declining church, drifting toward worldliness and the compromise of Biblical truth (1 Cor.14:3); (Matt. 23:31-38); (Luke 11:49); (Acts 7:51-52) if Prophets are not allowed to bring words of rebuke, and warning words, promoted by the spirit, words exposing sin and unrighteousness. (John 16:8-16). The church will become a place where the

vice of the spirit can no longer be heard. Ecclesiastical politics and worldly power will replace the spirit. (2 Tim. 4:3-5); (2 Pet. 2:1-3; 12-22). On the other hand, if the church, with its leaders, hears the voice of the prophets, it will be moved to renewed life, and fellowship with Christ. Sin will be forsaken, and the spirit's presence will be evident among the faithful. (1 Cor. 14:3); (1 Thess. 5:19-21); (Rev. 3:20-22).

PROPHETS

NAMES OF:

Enoch . . . . .Gen. 5:21,24

Noah . . . . .Gen. 9:25-27

Abraham . . . . .Gen. 20:1,7

Jacob . . . . .Gen. 49:1

Aaron . . . . .Ex. 7:1

Moses . . . . .Deut. 18:18

Joshua . . . . .1 Ki. 16:34

One Sent To Israel . . . . .Judg. 6:8-10

One Sent To Eli . . . . .1 Sam. 2:27-36

Samuel . . . . .1 Sam. 3:20

David . . . . .Acts 2:,25,30

Nathan . . . . .2 Sam. 7: 2

Zadok . . . . .2 Sam. 15:27

Gad . . . . .2 Sam. 24:11-14

Ahijah . . . . .1 Ki. 11:29

One Of Judah . . . . .1 Ki. 13:1

Iddo . . . . .2 Chr. 9:29

Shemaiah . . . . .2 Chr. 12:5,7,15

Azariah . . . . .2 Chr. 15:1-8

Hanani . . . . .2 Chr. 16:7-10

Jehu 1 Ki.16:1,7,12
Elijah 1 Ki.17:1
Elisha . . . . .1 Ki. 19:16
Micaiah . . . . .1 Ki. 22:7,8
Jonah . . . . .2 Ki. 14:25
Isaiah 2 Ki.19:2
Hosea . . . . .Hos. 1:1
Amos . . . . .Amos 1:1
Micah . . . . .Mic. 1:1
Oded . . . . .2 Chr. 28:9
Nahum . . . . .Nah. 1:1
Joel . . . . .Joel 1:1
Zephaniah .Zeph. 1:1
Jeduthun . . . . .2 Chr. 35:15
Jeremiah . . . . .2 Chr. 36:12,21
Habakkuk . . . . .Hab. 1:1
Obadiah . . . . .Obad. 1
Ezekiel . . . . .Ezek. 1:3
Daniel . . . . .Matt. 24:15
Haggai . . . . .Ezra 5:1; Zech. 1:1; Luke 1:67
Malachi Mal.1:1
John The Baptist . . . . .Luke 7:26-28
Agabus . . . . .Acts 11:28
Paul . . . . .1 Tim. 4:1
Peter . . . . .2 Pet. 2:1-2
John . . . . .Rev. 1:1

PROPHETS: INSPIRED MESSENGERS

(A). DESCRIBED AS:

God's Servants . . . . .Zech. 1:6

God's Messengers . . . . .2 Chr. 36:15

Holy Prophets . . . . .Luke 1:70

Holy Men . . . . .2 Pet. 1:21

Watchman . . . . .Ezek. 3:17

Prophets Of God . . . . .Ezra 5:2

(B). MESSAGE OF:

Centered In Christ . . . . .Luke 10:24

Interpreted By Christ . . . . .Luke 24:27,44

United In Testimony . . . . .Acts 3:21,24

Contains Grace And Salvation . . . . . . .1 Pet. 1:9-12

Abiding Revelation . . . . .Matt. 5:17,18

PROPHETS IN THE NEW TESTAMENT

(A). OFFICE OF; BASED UPON:

Christ's Prophetic Office . . . . .Deut. 18:15,18

Old Testament: . . . . .Joel 2:28

Prediction . . . . .Acts 2:28

Holy Spirit Coming . . . . .John 16:7,13

Divine Institution . . . . .1 Cor. 12:28

(B). FUNCTION OF:

Edify . . . . .Acts 15:32

Define God's Will . . . . .Acts 13:1-3

Predict The Future . . . . .Acts 21:10-11

PROPHETESS: A FEMALE PROPHET

(A). GOOD:
Miriam . . . . .Ex. 15:20-21
Deborah . . . . .Judg. 4:4-5
Huldah . . . . .2 Ki. 22:12-20
Isaiah's Wife .Is. 8:1-3
Anna . . . . .Luke 2:36
Daughters Of Philip . . . . .Acts 21:8-9
Prophecy Concerning . . . . .Joel 2:28

(B). FALSE:
Women's Of Judah . . . . .Ezek. 13:17
Noadiah . . . . .Neh. 6:14
Jezebel . . . . .Rev. 2:20

FALSE PROPHETS

(A). TEST OF:
Doctrine . . . . Is. 8:20
Prophecies . . . . .1 Ki. 13:1-32
Live . . . . .Matt. 7:15-16

(B). CHARATERISTICS OF:
Prophesy Peace . . . . .Jer. 23:17
Teach A Lie . . . . .Jer. 28:15
Pretend To Be True . . . . .Matt. 7:22-23
Teach Corruption . . . . .2 Pet. 2:10-22

(C). EXAMPLE OF:
Zedekiah . . . . .1 Ki. 22:11-12

Hananiah ....Jer. 28:1-17
In The Last Days ....Matt. 24:11

FALSE CHRIST

Christ Foretells Their Coming Matt.24:4
Christ Warns Against ....Mark 13:21-23

FALSE PASTOR

Selfish And Greedy ....Is. 56:10-12
Unmindful Of Flock ....Ezek. 34:2-4
Driving The Flock Away ....Acts 20:29-30

FALSE PROPHETS

(A). TEST OF:
Doctrine .... Is. 8:20
Prophecies ....1 Kings 13:1-32
Lives ....Matt. 7:15-16

(B). CHARACTERISTICS OF:
Prophesy Peace ....Jer. 23:17
Teach A Lie ....Jer. 28:15
Pretend To Be True ....Matt 7:22-23
Teach Corruption ....2 Pet. 2:10-22

(C). EXAMPLE OF:
Zedekiah ....1 King 22:11-12

Hananiah ....Jer. 28:1-17
In The Last Days ....Matt. 24:11

PROPHECY
INSPIRED FORETELLING OF EVENTS

(A). CHARACTERISTICS OF:
Authored By God ....Is. 41:22-23
Centered In Christ ....Luke 24:26-27, 44
Inspired By The Spirit ....2 Pet. 1:21
Not Of Private Interpretation ....2 Pet. 1:20
Always Relevant ....Rev. 22:10
Must Not Be Altered By Man ....Rev. 22:18-19

(B). TRUE; BASED ON:
Inspiration ....Mic. 3:8
Foreknowledge ....Is. 42:9

(C). FALSE; EVIDENCED BY:
Nonfullfillment ....Jer. 28:1-7
Peaceful Message ....Jer. 23:17-22
Apostasy From God 13:1-5
LyingJer. 23:25-34
Scoffing ....2 Pet. 3:3-4

(D). FULLFILLMENT OF:
Unconditional ....Ezek. 12:25-28
Sometime; Conditional ....Jonah 3:1-10
DatedDan. 9:24-27
Non-Literal ....Matt. 17:10-12
Unrecognized By Jews ....Acts 13:27-29

Interpretation Of; Needed . . . . .Luke 24:25-44
Often; Referred To . . . . .Matt. 1:22-23; 2:14-23

EVANGELIST

A person who travel from place to place, preaching the gospel.

Philip was one of the zealous evangelists of the early churches (Acts 21:8).

Evangelist

One Who Proclaims Good News

In the New Testaments, Evangelists were men of God, who were gifted, and commission by God; To proclaim the gospel (good news), of salvation to the unsaved, and to help establish a new work in a city. When proclaimed it always carries with it the offer and power of salvation.

(1) THE MINISTRY OF PHILIP THE EVANGELIST: (Acts 21:8) Gives A Clear Picture of the work of an evangelist according to the New Testament Pattern.

(A) Philip Preached The Gospel Of Christ . . . . .Acts 8:4-5, 3

(B) Many Were Saved And Baptized With Water . . . .Acts 8:6, 12

(C) Signs, Miracles, Healings, And Deliverance From Evil Spirits Accompanied His Preaching . . . . .Acts 8:6-7, 13

(D) He Was Concerned That New Converts Be Filled With The Holy Spirit .Acts 8:12-17; 2:38; 19:1-6

(2). THE EVANGELIST IS ESSENTIAL TO GOD'S PURPOSE
FOR THE CHURCH: The Church that fails to encourage and
support the Ministry of the Evangelist, will cease to gain converts
as God desires. It will become a static Church, devoid of growth,
and Missionary outreach. The Church that values the Spiritual gift
of the Evangelist, and maintains an earnest love, and care for the
lost, will proclaim the message of salvation, with convicing, and saving power. (Acts 2:14-41).

PASTORS

Pastors are called of God to perfect the saints and build up the body of Christ. (Eph. 4:11-13)

Pastors

Pastors Are Those Who Oversee

Pastors are those who oversees, and care for the spiritual needs of a local congregation. They are also called "Elders". And from Mi-le-'tus he sent to Eph'e-sus, and called the elders of the church. (Acts 20:17).

For this cause left I thee in Crete, that thou shouldest set in order the things that are wanting, and ordain elders in every city, as I appointed thee. (Tit. 1:5); An Overseer. (Tit. 1:7; 1 Tim. 3:1),

(1) a) An task of Pastors is to proclaim sound doctrine, reflute heresy. (Tit. 1:9-11).
 b) Teach God's word and excerise leadership in the local church. (1 Thess. 5:12).
 c) Be an example of purity and sound doctrine. (1 Tim. 3:1-5).
 d) And see to it that all believers remains in divine grace. (Tit. 2:7-8); (Heb.12:15); (Heb. 13:17); (1 Pet, 5:2).

Their task is described in (Acts 20:28-31). As safeguarding apostolic truth, and God's flock, by watching out for false doctrine and false teachers within the church, (See article on overseers and their duties).

Pastors function as shepherd, of which Jesus as the good shepherd is a model. (John 10:11-16).

(2) a). The New Testament pattern shows a plurality of Pastors directing the spiritual life of a local church. (Acts 20:28).

  b) Pastors were chosen not through politics or power plays, but through the spirit's wisdom, given to the body as it examined the candiates spiritual qualifications.

(3) a) Pastors are essential to God's purpose for His church. The church that fails to select godly and faithful pastors will cease to be governed according to the mind of the Spirit (see, 1Tim. 3:1-7). It will be a church left open to the destructive forces of Satan and the world (see, Acts 20:28-31), The preaching of the word will be distorted and the standards of the gospel lost (2Tim. 1:13-14). Members and families of the church will not be cared for according to God's purpose (1Tim. 4:6,12-16; 6:20-21)). Many will turn away from the truth and turn aside to myths (2Tim.4:4). On the other hand if godly pastors are appointed, believers will be nourished on the words of faith and sound doctrine and disciplined for the purpose of godliness (1Tim. 4:6-7). The church will be taught to persevere in the teaching of Christ and the apostles and thus ensure salvation for itself and those who hear (1Tim. 4:16); (2Tim. 2:2).

SHEPHERD, JESUS THE GOOD

(A) DESCRIBED PROPHETICALLY IN HIS:
Prophetic office (teaching) . . . . .Is. 40:10-11
Priestly Office (sacrifice) . . . . .Zech. 13:7
. . . . .Matt. 26:31

Kingly Office (ruling) . . . . .Ezek. 37:24

. . . . .Matt. 2:6

(B). DESCRIBED TYPICALLY AS:

Good . . . . .John 10:11, 14

Chief . . . . .1 Pet. 5:4

Great . . . . .Heb. 13:20

One . . . . .John 10:16

Gentle . . . . .Is. 40:11

Great Divider .Matt. 25:31-46

SHEPHERD: ONE WHO CARES FOR THE SHEEP

(A) DUTIES OF: TOWARD HIS FLOCK:

Defend . . . . .1 Sam. 17:34-36

Water . . . . .Gen. 29:2-10

Give Rest To . . . . .Jer. 33:12

Know . . . . .John 10:3-5

Number . . . . .Jer. 33:13

Secure Pasture for . . . . .Chr. 4:39-41

Search For The Lost . . . . .Ezek. 34:12-16

. . . . .Luke 15: 4-5

(B) GOOD, DESCRIBE AS:

Faithful . . . . .Gen. 31:38-40

Fearless . . . . .1 Sam. 17: 34-36

Unselfish . . . . .Luke 15:3-6

Considerate . . . . .Gen. 33: 13-14

Believing . . . . .Luke 2: 8-20

(C) BAD, DESCRIBE AS:
Unfaithful . . . . .Ezek. 34:1-10
Cowardly . . . . .John 10: 12-13
Selfish . . . . .Isa. 56: 11-12
Ruthless . . . . .Ex. 2:17,19
Unbelieving .Jer. 56:6

(D) DESCRIPTIVE OF:
God . . . . .Ps. 78:52-53
Christ . . . . .Heb. 13:20
Joshua Num.27:16-23
David . . . . .2 Sam. 5:2
Judges . . . . .1 Chr. 17:6
National Leaders . . . . .Jer. 49:19
Cyrus . . . . .Is. 44:28
Jewish Leaders . . . . .Matt. 9:36
Church Leaders . . . . .1 Pet. 5:2

MORAL QUALIFICATIONS FOR OVERSEERS

(1 Tim. 3:1-2):
Here is a trustworthy saying: If anyone sets his heart on being an overseer, he desire a noble task, now the overseers must be above repoach, the husband of but one wife, temperate self-controlled, respectable, hospitable, able to teach.

If a man wants to be an overseer, one who has Pastoral oversight (a Pastor), He desires an important work. (1 Tim. 3:1). However, such peoples must have that desire confirmed by God's word, (1 Tim. 3:1-10); (1 Tim. 4:1)), and the church. (1 Tim. 3:10), For God has established for the church certain specific qualifications. Any professed call of God to do the works of a Pastor must be tested by the members of the church according to the bibicial standard of (1 Tim. 3:1-13; 4:12); (Tit. 1:5-9). The church must not endorse any person for ministerial work based solely on his desire, education, burden, or alleged vision, or call. The church today has no right to diminish the requirements that God set forth by the Holy Spirit. They stand as absolutes and must be followed for the sake of God's name, His Kingdom, and the credibility of the high office of Overseer.

1) The standards listed for Overseer are primarily moral and spiritual. The proven charcter of those who seek leadership in the church is more important than personality, preaching gifts, administrative abilities, or academic accomplishments. The focal point of the qualifications falls on behavior that has perserved in Godly wisdom, right choices, and personal Holiness. The spiritual history of the person who desires the office of overseer, has to first be tested. (1 Tim. 3:10). Thus the Holy Spirit sets forth the high standard that the candidates must be a believer who has steadfastly adhered to Jesus Christ, and His principles of righteousness, and who can therefore serve as a role model of faithfulness, truth, honesty, and purity. In other words, His character must reflect Christ's, teaching in (Matt. 25:21)," that being faithful with a few things," leads to a position of being in charge of many things.

2) Above all, Christain teachers must set an example for the believers. (1 Tim. 4:12); (1 Pet. 5:3). Their christian life and steadfast faith can be set before the congregation as preeminently worthy of imitation.
   a) Overseers must demonstrate the highest example of perserverance in godliness, faithfulness, purity in the face of temptation, and loyality to, and love for Christ, and gospel. (1 Tim. 4:12,15).

b) God's peoples must learn christains ethics and true godliness, not only from the word of God, but also from examples of pastors who live according to apostolic standards. Pastors who quality of life is an illustration of the faith are absolutely essential in God's plan for christains leadership. To throw aside the principles of having godly leadership that has set an unblemished pattern for those of the church to follow, is to ignore scripture's clear thinking. Pastors must must be peoples whose faithfulness to Christ can be set forth as a pattern or examples. (1 Cor. 11:1); (Philp. 3:17); (1 Thess. 1:6; 3:7,9); (2 Thess. 1:13).

3) The Holy Spirit regards the believer's leadership at home, marraige, and family relationship as of the highest importance. (1 Tim. 3:2, 4-5); (Tit. 1:6). The overseer must be an example to the family of God, especially in his faithfulness to his wife and childrens. After all if he has failed in this realm, how can he take care of God's church? (1 Tim. 3:5). He must be the husband of but one wife. (1 Tim. 3:2). The phase defends the position that a candidate for the office of an overseer should be a believer who has remained morally faithful to his wife. The literal translation of the Greek (mias-gunaikos; as attributive genitive) is a one woman man, the faithful husband of his wife. This mean that the candidate must be a person who gives evidence of being faithful in this all-important area, perservering moral faithfulness to one's wife and family, is required for any one desiring to be a leader and an example in the church.

4) Consequently, person within the church who become guilty of serious sin or moral transgressions have disqualified themselves from the office of pastor and from any position of high leadership in the local church. (1 Tim. 3:8-12). Such peoples may be abundantly pardoned by God's grace, but they have lost the capacity to serve as

models of unfailing perseverance in faith, love, purity, and sound doctrine. (1 Tim. 4:11-16); (Tit. 1:9).

5) Futhermore, (1 Tim. 3:2,7) sets forth the principle that an overseer who throws aside his loyalty to God and His word, and His fidelity to wife and family must be removed from the office an overseer. He cannot thereafter be regarded as above reproach (1Tim. 3:2) concerning one among God's peoples who commits adultery, God's word states that His shame will never be wiped away (Prov. 6:33).

6) This does not mean that God or the church will not forgive. God will indeed forgive any sin, listed in (1Tim. 3:1-13) if they is godly sorrowful and repentance for that sin let it be clear that such a person maybe mercifully forgiven and restored in His relationship to God, and the Church. However, what the Holy Spirit is stating is that there are some sins so grave that the disgrace and shame (i.e., reproach), of that sin will remain with an individual, even after forgiveness. (2 Sam. 12:9-14).

7) But what about King David? His continuation as Israel's King in spite of his sins of adultery and murder (2 Sam. 11:1-21; 12:9-15) is sometime viewed as biblical justification for one's continuance as an overseer even though he has violated the above mentioned standards. This comparison however is faulty on several counts.

   a) The office of the King of Israel under the old covenant and that of spiritual overseer of the church not only David but also many kings who were exceptionally wicked to remain as Kings of Israel leadership of the New Testament Church that was purchased with the blood of Jesus Christ required much higher spiritual standards.

   b) According to God's revelation and requirements in the New Testament, David would not have qualified for the office of an overseer in a New Testament Church. He had multiple wives, was guilty of martial unfaithfulness, failed miserably to manage his own household, and was a murder and a violent man of bloodshed, note to that because of his sin. David remained under God's punishment for the rest of his life. (2 Sam. 12:9-12).

8) Today's churches must not turn from the righteous require-ments for an overseer set forth by God in the original revelation of the Apostles. Instead the church must require from its leaders the highest standard of holiness, preseverance in faithfulness to God and His word, and godly living. They are to be earnestly prayed for, encouraged and supported, while they set an exam-ple for the believers in speech, in life, in love, in faith and in purity. (1 Tim. 4:12).

OVERSEERS AND THEIR DUTIES

(Acts 20:28); Take heed therefore unto yourselves, and to all flocks over the which the Holy Ghost hath made you overseers, Be shepherds of the church of God: which he hath purchased "(bought)" with his own blood.

No church can function without designated leaders. Thus as, (Acts14:23), indicates certain individuals were appointed to the office of Elders or Overseers by spirit-filled believers who sought God's will through prayers and fasting. In accordance with the spiritual qualifica-tions sent down by the Holy Spirit in (1 Tim. 3:1-7); (Tit. 1:5-9). Ul-timately, therefore it is the spirit who makes someone an overseer or the church Paul's speech, to the Ephesian Elders. (Acts 20:18-35) is a classic passage giving scriptural principles on how to function as an overseers within the visible church.

PROMOTING THE FAITH:

1) One of the mayor duties of an overseer is to feed the sheep, by teaching God's word. They must always keep in mind that the flock given to them, is no other than the peoples that God has purchased for himself with his son's precious blood. (Acts 20:28); (1 Cor. 6:20); (1 Pet. 1:19; 2:9); (Rev. 5:9).

2) In (Acts 20:19-27) Paul describes how He served as a shepherd of the church of Ephesus; he has declared the whole will of God by faithfully warning and teaching the Ephesian Christians. (Acts 20:27). Consequently he is able to say; I am pure "(innocent)" of the blood of all men. (Acts 20:26).

   Overseers today must like wise declare to their churches God's whole will. They must preach the word correct, rebuke, and encourage with great patience, and careful instruction, (2 Tim. 4:2); and refuse to be preachers who seek to please peoples and say only what they want to hear. (2 Tim 4:3)

Guarding the faith the true pastors must diligently protect the sheeps from their enemies. Paul knows that in the church's future, satan will raise up false teachers from within the churches and infiltrate God's flock, from the outside with imposters who adhere to unbibical doctrine, worldly thoughts, and pagans and humanistic ideas. Both will destroy the bibical faith of God's peoples. Paul calls them salvage wolves, meaning that they are strong, difficult to handle, ravenous, and dangerous. (Acts 20:29); (Matt. 10:16). Such individuals will draw peoples away from Christ's teachings and toward themselves and their distorted gospel. Paul's urgent plea (Acts 20:25-31), places a solemn obligation on all church leaders to guard the church and oppose all who would distort the fundamental revelation of New Testament faith.

OVERSEERS AND THEIR DUTIES

1) The true church consist of only those who by Christ's grace, and the fellowship of the Holy Spirit are faithful to the Lord Jesus Christ, and the word of God. Therefore, as a mayor aspect of guarding God's church. Church leaders must discipline correct in love (Eph. 4:15), and firmly refute (2 Tim. 4:1-4); (Tit. 1:9-11); all within the church who distort the truth (Acts 20:30), by teaching things contrary to God's word and apostolic witness.

2) Church Leaders, Pastors, of Local Congregations and Administrative Officials, do well to remember that the Lord Jesus has made them responsible for the blood of all persons under their care. (Acts 20:26-27); (Ezek. 3:20-21); if leaders fail to declare and perform God's whole purpose for the church (Acts 20:27), especially in the area of keeping watch over the flock. (Acts 20:28). They will not be innocent of the blood of all men. (Acts 20:26); (Ezek. 34:1-10). Instead God will hold them guilty of the blood of all those who are lost, because of the leaders refusal to protect the flock from those who weaken and distort the word. (2 Tim. 1:14); (Rev. 2:2).

3) Exercising discipline with regard to Theological Doctrinal, and moral matters by and upon those who are responsible for the church's direction is especially important. Purity of doctrine and life and adherence to the inerrance of scriptures must be carefully guarded in colleges, bible schools, seminaries, publishing institutions, and all organizational structures of the church. (2 Tim. 1:13-14).

4) The main issue here is one's attitude toward divinely inspired scriptures, which Paul called the word of his grace (Acts 20:32). False Teachers, Pastors and Leaders will attempt to weaken the authority

of the Bible by their subversive teachings and unbibicial principles, by rejecting the full authority of God's word. They deny that the Bible is true and trust worthy in all that it teaches. (Acts 20:28-31); (Gal. 1:6); (1 Tim. 4:1); (2 Tim. 3:8), these peoples, for the sake of the church, must be disciplined and removed from the fellowship. (2 John 1:9-11); (Gal. 1:9).

5) The Church that fails to share the Holy Spirit's burning concern for church purity, (Acts 20:18-35), refuses to maintain a firm stand for the truth, and refrains from disciplining those who undermine the authority of God's word, will soon cease to exist as a church according to New Testament norm (Acts 12:5). It will become guiltily of apostasy from the original revelation of Christ and the Apostles, sliding further and further from the New Testament purpose, power, and life.

PREACHERS/TEACHERS

Pastors and Teachers are persons, who master and communicates knowledge or religious truth to others. Whose skills and ministry are needed in the church. (Eph. 4:11-12).

Teachers

TEACHERS: Teachers are those who have a special, God-given gift to clarify, expound and proclaim God's word in order to build up the body of Christ. (Eph. 4:12).

1) The special task of teachers is to guard, by the help of the Holy Spirit, the gospel entrusted to them (2 Tim. 1:11-14). They are faithfully to point the church to Biblical revelation and to the original message of Christ and the apostles, and to persevere in this task.

2) The principal purpose of Biblical teaching is to perserve truth and to produce holiness by leading Christ's body into an uncompromising commitment to the godly lifestyle set forth in God's word. Scriptures states that the goal of Christain instruction is "love, which comes from a pure heart and a good conscience and a sincere faith" (1 Tim. 1:5). Thus, the evidence of Christians learning is not just in what one knows, but how one lives-i.e., the manifestation of love, purity, faith, godliness.

3) Teachers are essential to God's purpose for His church. The church that rejects or refuses to hear those teachers and theologians who remain faithful to Scriptural revelation will stop being concern about the genuineness of the Biblical message and the correct in-

terpretation of the original teaching of Christ and the apostles. The church in which such teachers and theologians remain silent will not continue steadfast in truth. New winds of doctrine will be uncritically accepted, and religious experience and human ideas, rather than revealed truths, will be the ultimate guide to the church's doctrine, standards and practices. On the other hand, the church that listens to godly teachers and theologians will have its teaching and practices measured by the original and fundamental testimony of the gospel, its false ideas exposed and purity of Christ's original message handed down to its children. God's inspired Word will become the test of all teaching, and the church will be ever reminded that the spirit's inspired Word is ultimate truth and authority, and as such, stands over the churches and their institutions.

TEACHING; TEACHERS

(A) THOSE CAPABLE OF:

Parents . . . . .Deut. 11:19

Levities . . . . .Lev. 10:11

Ancestors . . . . .Jer. 9:14

Disciples . . . . .Matt. 28:19

Church Leaders . . . . .Tit. 2:3

Nature . . . . .1 Cor. 11:14

(B) SIGNIFICANCE OF:

Combined With Preaching . . . . .Matt. 4:23

Divine Calling . . . . .Eph. 4:11

Necessary For Officers . . . . .Tim. 3:2

Necessary For Ministers . . . . .Tim. 2:24-26

From House To House . . . . .Acts 20:20

By Catechizing . . . . .Gal. 6:6

Not Granted To Women . . . . .Tim. 2:12

(C) AUTHORITY OF; IN DIVINE THINGS:

Derived From Christ . . . . .Matt. 28:19

Empowered By The Spirit . . . . .John 14:26

Taught By God . . . . .Is. 54:13

originates In Revelation . . . . .Gal. 1:12

(D) OBJECTS OF; IN DIVINE THINGS, CONCERNING:

God's Way . . . . .Ps. 27:11

God's Path . . . . .Ps. 25:4-5

God's Law . . . . .Ps. 119:12,26,66

God's Will . . . . .Ps. 143:10

Holiness . . . . .Tit. 2:12

Spiritual Truths . . . . .Heb. 8:12

(E) PERVERSION OF; BY:

False Prophets . . . . .Is. 9:15

False Priests .Mic. 3:11

Traditionalists .Matt. 15:9

False Teachers . . . . .1 Tim. 4:1-3

Judaizers . . . . .Acts 15:1

False Believers . . . . .2 Tim. 4:3-4

TEACHABLENESS: A WILLINGNESS TO LEARN

(A) CHARACTERIZED BY:

Humility . . . . .Matt. 11:29 .

Willingness To Learn . . . . .Acts 8: 27-37

(B) ILLUSTRATED BY:

Jesus As A Child . . . . .Luke 2:46-47

Mary . . . . .Luke 10:38-42

Cornelius . . . . .Acts 10:30-33

PREACH, ...PREACHING, ...PROCLAIMING THE GOSPEL

PREACH:

1) To speak in public on religious matters, give a sermon.

2) To give moral or religious advice, especially in a tiresome manner.

PREACHING:

1) To urge or expound as by Preaching.

2) To deliver (a sermon), Preaching.

PREACHER:

1) A person who Preaches, especially a clergyman.

CLERGYMAN:

1) A member of the Clergy; Minister, Priest, etc..

CLERGY:

1) Men Ordained for religious service, as Ministers, Priests, etc..

PREACH, ...PREACHING,...PROCLAIMING THE GOSPEL

(A) OF THE GOSPEL:

Necessity Of . . . . .1 Cor. 9:16

Without Change . . . . .1 Cor. 9:18

Extent Of, To All . . . . .Col. 1:23

Only One . . . . .Gal. 1:8-9
Centers In The Cross . . . . .1 Cor. 1:23
Preaches Importance In . . . . .Rom. 10:14-15

(B) ATTITUDES TOWARD:

Accepted . . . . .Luke 11:32
Rejected . . . . .2 Pet. 2:4-5
Not Perfected By . . . . .Heb. 4:2
Perverted Gal.1 6-9
Contentious About . . . . .Phil. 1:15-18
Counted Foolishness . . . . .1 Cor. 1:18-21
Ridiculed . . . . .Acts 17: 16-18
Not Ashamed Of . . . . .Rom. 1:15-16

FALSE TEACHERS

(Mark 13:22); For false christs and false prophets shall rise, and shall show signs and wonders (miracles), to seduce (deceive), if it were possible, even the elect.

{DESCRIPTION}:
Belivers today must be aware that within the churches there may be Ministers of God's word who are of the same spirit and life as the corrupt teachers of God's Law in Jesus day (Matt. 24:11,24). Jesus warns that not everyone who professes Christ is a true believer, nor are all christains Writers, Missionaries, Pastors, Evangelists, Teachers, Deacons, and Workers, what they claim to be.

1) These Ministers will on the outside appear to peoples, as righeous (Matt 13:28). They comes in sheep's clothing (Matt. 7:15). They may base their message solidly on God's word and proclaim high

righteous standards. They may appear sincerely concerned for God's work and Kingdom and show great interest in the salvation of the lost, while professing love for all peoples. They may appear to be great Ministers of God commendable spiritual leaders anointed by the Holy Spirit. They may have great success, and multitudes may fellow them, (see Matt. 7:21-23; 24:11.24); (2 Cor. 11:13-15).

2) Nevertheless, these peoples are like the Pharisees of old, away from the crowds and in their hidden lives, they are given over to greed, and self-indulgence (Matt. 23:25); full of dead men's bones and everything unclean (Matt. 23:27). Full of hypocrisy and wickedness (Matt. 23:28).

3) These imposters gain a place of influence in the church in two ways.
   a) Some false teachers/preachers begin their ministry in sincerity, truth, purity, and genuine faith in Christ. Then because of their pride and their own immortal desires, personal commitments to, and love for Christ gradually die. Consequently they are severed from God's Kindgom (1 Cor. 6:9-10); ((Gal. 5:19-21); (Eph. 5:5-6), and becomes instruments of satan while disguising themselves as Ministers of righteousness (see, 2 Cor. 11:15).

   b) Other false Teachers/Preachers have never been genuine believers in Christ. Satan has planted them within the churches from the very beginning of their Ministry (Matt. 13:24-28; 36-43), using their ability and charisma and aiding in their success. His strategy is to place in influential positions so that they can undermine the genuine work of Christ. If they are discovered or exposed Satan knows that great damage will come to the gospel and that the name of Christ will be put to open shame.

FALSE TEACHERS

Testing: Jesus warned His Disciples fourteen times in the Gospels to watch out for leaders who would mislead (Matt. 7:15; 16:6,11; 24:4,24); (Mark 4:24; 8:15; 12:38-40; 13:5); (Luke 12:1; 17:23; 20:46; 21:8)., Elsewhere believers are exhorted to test Teachers, Preachers, and Leaders in the Church (1 Thess. 5:21; 1 John 4:1). The following steps can be taken in testing false teachers or false phophets:

1) DISCERN CHARACTER: Do they have diligent prayer lives, and do they show a sincere and pure devotion to God? Do they manifest the fruit of the spirit (Gal. 5:22-23), love sinners (John 3:16), hate wickedness and love righteousness (Heb. 1:9 note), and cry out aganist sin (Matt. 23:1-39); (Luke 2:18-20)?

2). DISCERN MOTIVES: True Christian Leaders will seek to do four things:
    (a) Honor Christ (2 Cor. 8; 23); (Phil. 1:20).
    (b) Lead the Church into santification (Acts 26:18); (1 Cor. 6:8); (2 Cor. 6:16-18).
    (c) Save the lost (1 Cor. 9:19-22).
    (d) Proclaim and defend the gospel of Christ and the Aspotles (Phil. 1:16); (Jude 1:3).

3) Test fruits in life and message. The fruits of false preachers will often consist in converts not totally committed to all of God's word (Matt. 7:16).

4) Discern level of reliance on scripture. This is a key issue. Do they believe and teach that the original writing of both the Old Testament and New Testament are fully inspired by God, and that we

are to submit to all its teaching (2 John 9-11)? if not, we can be sure that they and their message are not from God.

5) Finally, test integrity with respect to the Lord's money. Do they refuse to take large amounts for themselves, handle all finances with integrity and responsibility, and seek to promote God's work in ways consistent with New Testament standards for leaders (1 Tim. 3:3; 6:9-10)? It must be understood that in spite of all, that faithful believers do in evaluating a person's life and message. There will still be false teachers within the churches who, with Satan's help, remains undetected until God determines to expose those persons for what they are.

MINISTERS

To "preach the word" and perform duty as God's servant. (2 Tim.4:2-5)

Duties of Ministers

TO PREACH TRUE DOCTRINE

(1 Cor. 1:23); But we preach Christ crucified unto the Jews a stumbling block, and unto the Greeks foolishness, (1 Cor. 1:24). But unto them which are called, both Jews and Greeks, Christ the power of God, and the wisdom of God.

(1 Cor. 2:1-5); And, I brethren, when I came to you, came not with excellency of speech or of wisdom, declaring unto you the testimony of God. (v2.) For I determined not to know any thing among you, save Jesus Christ, and him crucified. (v3.) And I was with you in weakness, and in fear, and in much trembling. (v4.) And my speech and my preaching was not with enticing words of man's wisdom, but in demonstration of the Spirit and power: (v5.) That your faith should not stand in the wisdom of men, but in the power of God.

(2 Cor. 3:9-13); For we are labourers together with God: ye are God's husbandry, ye are God's building. (v10.); According to the grace of God which is given unto me, as a wise masterbuilder, I have laid the foundation, and another buildeth thereon. But let every man take heed how he buildeth thereupon. (v11.); For other foundation can no man lay than that is laid, which is Jesus Christ. (v12.); Now if any man build upon this foundation gold. silver, precious stones, wood, hay, stubble; (v13.) Every man's work shall be made manifest: for the day shall declare it, because it shall be revealed by fire; and the fire shall try every man's work of what sort it is.

CHRIST'S COMMISSION TO MINISTERS

(Matt. 28:19-20); Go ye therefore, and teach all nations, baptizing them in the name of the Father, and of the Son, and of the Holy Ghost:

(v20). Teaching them to observe all things whatsoever I have commanded you: and, lo, I am with you always, even unto the end of the world. Amen.

(John 4:35); Say not ye, There are yet four months, and then cometh harvest? behold, I say unto you, Lift up your eyes, and look on the fields; for they are white already to harvest.

CHARACTER AND QUALIFICATIONS OF A MINISTER

KNOWLEDGE AND DISCRETION

(Luke 6:39); And he spake a parable unto them, Can the blind lead the blind: shall they not both fall into the ditch?

(2 Cor. 11:12-13); But what I do, that I will do, that I may cut off occasion from them which desire occasion; that wherein they glory, they may be found even as we.

(v13); For such are false apostles, deceitful workers, transforming themselves into the apostles of Christ.

(Gal. 2:2); And I went up by revelation, and communicated unto them that gospel which I preach among the Gentiles, but privately to them which were of reputation, lest by any means I should run, or had run, in vain.

MINISTERS: ONE WHO SERVES

(A) DESCRIPTIVE OF:

Assistant . . . . .Acts 13:5

Court Attendants . . . . .1 Ki. 10:5

Angels . . . . .Ps. 103:20

Priest And Levites . . . . .Joel 1;9,13

Servant . . . . .Matt. 20:22-27

Magistrate . . . . .Rom. 13:4,6

Christ . . . . .Rom. 15:8

Christ's Messengers . . . . .1 Cor. 3:5

False Teachers . . . . .2 Cor. 11:15

(B) CHRISTIAN, QUALIFICATION OF:

Able To Teach . . . . .1 Tim. 3:2

Courageous . . . . .Acts 20:22-24

Diligent . . . . .1 Cor. 15:10

Faithful . . . . .Rom. 15:17-19

Impartial . . . . .1 Tim. 5:21

Industrious . . . . .2 Cor. 10:12-16

Meek . . . . .2 Tim. 2:25

Obedient . . . . .Acts 16:9-10

Persevering . . . . .2 Cor. 11:23-33

Prayerful . . . . .Acts 6:4

Sincere . . . . .2 Car 4:1-2

Spirit Filled . . . . .Acts 1:8

Studious . . . . .1 Tim. 4:13,15

Sympathetic . . . . .Heb. 5:2

Temperate . . . . .1 Cor. 9:25-27

Willing . . . . .1 Pet. 5:2

Worthy Of Imitation . . . . .1 Tim. 4:12

(C) SINS TO AVOID:
Arrogance . . . . .1 Pet. 5:3
Contentiousness . . . . .Tit. 1:7
Discouragement . . . . .2 Cor. 4:8-9
Insincerity . . . . .Phil. 1:15-16
Perverting The Truth . . . . .Cor. 11:3-15
Unfaithfulness . . . . .Matt. 24: 48-51

(D) DUTIES OF: PREACH:
Gospel . . . . .1 Cor. 1:17
Christ Crucified . . . . .1 Cor. 1:23
Christ's Riches . . . . .Eph. 3:8-12
Feed The Church . . . . .John 21:15-17
Edify The Church . . . . .Eph. 4:12
Pray For Peoples . . . . .Col. 1:9
Teach . . . . .2 Tim. 2:2
Exhort . . . . .Tit. 1:9
Rebuke . . . . .Tit. 2:15
Warn Of Apostasy . . . . .2 Tim. 4:2-5
Comfort . . . . .2 Cor. 1:4-6
Win Souls . . . . .1 Cor. 9:19-23

(E) ATTITUDE OF BELIEVERS TOWARD:
Pray For . . . . .Eph. 6:18-20
Follow The Example Of . . . . .1 Cor. 11:1
Obey . . . . .1 Thess. 5:12-13
Esteem Highly . . . . .1 Cor. 4: 1-2
Provided For . . . . .1 Cor. 9:6-18

EXHORTATION
ENCOURAGING OTHERS TO COMMENDABLE CONDUCT

(A) OBJECT OF:
Call To Repentance . . . . .Luke 3:17-18
Continue In The Faith . . . . .Acts 14:22
Convict Gainsayers . . . . .Tit. 1:9
Warn The Unruly . . . . .1 Thess. 5:14
Encourage Soberness . . . . .Tit. 2:6
Strenghten Godliness . . . . .Thess. 4:1-6
Stir Up Liberality . . . . .2 Cor. 9:5-7

(B) OFFICE OF:
Commended . . . . .Rom. 12:8
Part Of The Ministry . . . . .Tit, 2:15
Needed In Time . . . . .Tim. 4:2-5

(C) NATURE OF:
Daily Duty . . . . .Heb. 3:13
For Holiness . . . . .1 Thess. 2:3
Worthy Of Reception . . . . .Heb. 13:22
Belongs To All . . . . .Heb. 10:25
Special Need Of . . . . .Jude 1:3-4

THE INSPIRATION AND AUTHORITY OF SCRIPTURE

(2 Tim. 3:16-17); All scripture is given by inspiration of God, and is profitable for doctrine, for reproof, for correction, for instruction in righteousness. (v17); That the man of God may be perfect, thoroughly furnished unto all works.

Scripture as used in (2 Tim. 3:16), refers primarily to the Old Testament writing(2 Tim. 3:15). There is indication, however, that is about the time Paul wrote 2 Timothy. Some New Testament writings were already viewed as inspired and authoriture scriptures (1 Tim. 5:18), which quotes (Luke 10:7); (2 Pet.3:15-16), for us today scripture refers to the authoritativewriting of both the Old Testament and New Testament the Bible. They are God's original message to humanity and the only infallible witness to God's saving activity for all peoples.

1) Paul affirms that all scripture is "God-breathed" < GK theopneustos from two greek words theos, meaning God, and pneo meaning to breathe. Scriptures is the very life and word of God, down to the very words of the original manuscripts. The Bible is without error, absolutely true, trustworthy and infallible. This is true not only when it speaks of salvation, ethical values and morality but it is also without error on all subjects about which it speaks including history and the cosmos (2 Pet. 1:20-21); note also the attitude of the Psalmist toward scripture in Psalm 119.

2) Jesus Christ taught that scripture is God's inspired word to even the smallest detail(Matt. 5:18). He also affirmed that all He said be recieved from the father and its true, (John 5:19,30,-31; 7:16; 8:26). He futher spoke of revelation yet to come (i e, the truth revealed in the New Testament) from the Holy Spirit through the Apostle (John 14:16-17; 15:26-27; 16:13).

3) To deny the full inspiration of holy scripture, therfore is to set aside the fundamental witness of Jesus Christ. (Matt. 5:18; 15:3-6); (Luke 16:7; 24:25-27, 44-45); (John 10:35), the Holy Spirit (John 15:26; 16:13); 1 Cor. 2:12-13); (1 Tim. 4:1), and the Apostles (2 Tim. 3:16); (2 Pet. 1:20-21). Futhermore, to limit or disregard its inerrancy is to impair its divine authority.

4) In His work of inspiration by His spirit, God, while not voilating the personality of the writers, moved on them in such a waymthat they wrote without error (2 Tim. 3:16); (2 Pet. 1:20-21), see (1Cor. 2:12-13, notes).

5) The inspired word of God is the expression of God's wisdom and character and is therefore able to give wisdom and spiritual life through faith in Christ (Matt. 4:4); (John 6:63); (2Tim. 3:15); (1Pet. 2:12).

6) The Bible is God's infallible true witness to His saving activing for humanity in Christ Jesus. For words or declarations of religious institutions are equal to its authority.

7) All doctrines mommentaries interpretations, explanations and traditions must be judged and legistimized by the words and message in scripture.

8) God's word must be recieved, believed, and obeyed as the final authoritybin all things pertaining to life and godliness (Matt. 5:17-19); (John 14:21; 15:10); (2Tim. 3:15-16), it must be used in the church as the final authority in all matters for teaching, rebuking, correcting and training in righteous living (2Tim. 3:16-17). One cannot submit to Christ's leadership without submitting to God's words as the ultimate authority (John 8:31-32, 37).

9) The bible can only be understood when we are in a right relationship to the Holy Spirit. It is He who opens our minds to understand its meaning and give us the inward witness of its authority see (1Cor. 2:12).

10) We must use God's inspired words to conquer the power of sin, satan and the world in our lives (Matt. 4:4); (Eph. 6:12-17); (James 1:21).

11) Scriptures must be loved, treasured and guarded by all church members who see it as God's only truth for a lost and dying world. We must safeguard its doctrines by faithfully adhering to its teaching, proclaiming its saving message, entrusting it to reliable peoples, and defending it aganist all who would distort or destroy its eternal truths (see Philip 1:16); (2Tim. 1:13-14); (2Tim. 2:2); (Jude 3).

12) Finally we should note that in errant inspiration applies only to the original writing of the Biblical Books thus, whenever one finds in scripture something that appears to be in error, rather than assuming that the writer made a mistake, one should remember that these possibilities exist. With great regard to any apparent problem:

   a) The existing copies of the original manuscript may not be totally accurate.
   b) The present-day translation of the Hebrew or Greek Biblical text may be faulty: or
   c) Ones understanding or interpretation of the biblical text may be inadequate or incorrect.

CPSIA information can be obtained
at www.ICGtesting.com
Printed in the USA
BVHW041833110422
633997BV00012B/373